Folk Writing by an Internet Person

Volume 2 of *My Autobiography is My Manifesto*

Neon Burrito Publishing

Shawn Michael Sullivan

We notice a car driving through a gas station parking lot to cut a street corner and my mother tells me, Just imagine what it would be like if everyone did that.

A child in the passenger seat, I begin to imagine what she asked me to imagine, since I closely listen to my sage mother: and I conclude that not everyone should do that, since a parking lot is not for that.

I write nonfiction, and one who believes that fiction is the road to writing might read nonfiction and consider themselves a witness to a person driving through a gas station parking lot to cut a street corner, the same as one who believes that nonfiction is the road to writing might read fiction and consider themselves a witness to a person driving through a gas station parking lot to cut a street corner, but I think they are both wrong, and I think they are both right, because I think that every book takes place in the land of words.

In word land, when my belly is a balloon, and I fall down, you hear my stomach pop: uh-oh. Now you're an ambulance driver, now you're an airplane pilot, now we're on a cloud island, and finally I'm in a hospital bed, the hospital looks like a castle. Thank you. Anything is possible and we're in this together.

If someone told me that writing books about my life doesn't require an ounce of imagination, I would consider that aggressive perspective unmitigated bullshit.

I am suggesting: under the circumstances of being a typical person blessed with being alive, if your life doesn't inspire your imagination that's a personal problem I don't need.

Here I am unfurling myself before you as a literary house of mirrors. Here are the words to the fourteenth book I've written, directly following a poetry collection that consisted of ten poems by me and two friends—thirty total poems—titled *The Mystery of Everything Everywhere*. I had been permitted to select the title and, honestly, it was inspired by the titles of Nancy Drew books.

How outrageous: this book is being written while a global pandemic persists at the beginning of 2021. What happened was: many of us people alive had expected science and human understanding to have advanced along far enough for this kind of pandemic to not happen, but then it did. Shit. Major shitstorm, which term also applies to colonialism, the patriarchy, and white supremacy.

I do not live in the future, I live at a point in time. Human reality is not the same now as it was one hundred years ago, and that will be true one hundred years from now, too. I want to write a book from a fuller perspective of human development, but here I am when I am, and my life is also like this: I'll know it best at its end. I keep waiting to see what I'm learning, and I keep discovering how I'm growing—every time I think I'm fully grown, I grow again.

Growing to a certain extent: for the past nine years I have lived in a two-bedroom apartment off of Fairfax Avenue, in Los Angeles, California. This is the same apartment I lived in while writing *Volume One* of *My Autobiography Is My Manifesto*, along with every other published and unpublished book of mine. When I moved in here, it was hilarious to me that my roommate had me sign the lease. I was so young and foolish of the future, such a dumbass, that I thought I would be gone from here in under a year or so.

.

Hahahahaha.

Almost dying of laughter before inhaling to regain composure: how wrong my expectations about life can be.

Various truth bombs that provide further frames of reference: my roommate initially moved in here six years prior to me, with a fraternal twin brother who has his own place now. Born in San Diego, a graduate of USC (film degree), both my roommate and his twin brother work in the entertainment industry—reality television. I consider the little I know about my roommate plenty, while wishing him the best in a theoretical sense. I vehemently treasure our independent lives. And he can be rude to me because I can be rude to him, although manners do not permit me to murder him (except in my daily imagination). On occasion we are kind to each other, too.

Not that I unfailingly achieve this, but my social goal with any person tends to be a dance beneath interior mountains of frustration. And although this is not so easy on certain days, it *is possible* for one to lift a mountain of frustration within them, and dance beneath it, despite it also being possible for one to feel crushed by the mountain of frustration within them.

Of course I am mentioning vaguely-interesting things I tend to mention: life is a lot. There are copious things to consider in terms of whatever I do and wherever I am, along with whatever I don't do and wherever I am not: relevant details about superficial and deeper implications, and grand mental meanings, plus grand exterior meanings: grand meanings fucking everywhere. Reality is so dope it can feel overwhelming on occasion. The abundance of possibility can feel both ethereal and suffocating.

My core existence is random: born in Southern Ohio during the 1980s, I am an out-of-wedlock accident between a truck driver and a grocery store manager. From many perspectives I am not worth mentioning, which I consider worth mentioning, because I think that is interesting.

Scientifically speaking in Pacific Standard Time, I began writing this book at three in the afternoon on my thirty-seventh birthday, although this book first entered my thoughts on the previous evening, while I strolled down Fairfax Avenue. I don't have a perfect memory but I write down some many things, and I plain remember a few things, which can later inspire me to write about them, such as when I am now writing about being a sixteen-year-old who took a vacation to visit his sister in Laguna Beach, California.

My half-sister—although I never call her that, and she never calls me her half-brother, although she called me half a brother after I introduced this topic to a conversation we once had, anyway—she moved from Ohio to California well before me and my mother. Eleven years older than me, my sister was married with three kids by the time my mother and I arrived in this dream state that is a real place.

And as a sixteen-year-old visiting his sister in California, I used a cable modem to chat on a videogame message board whenever the opportunity presented itself, because sure I had heard about cable modems back in Ohio, but I didn't have one—I had dial-up—so I was legit stoked about hanging out with my internet friends across a faster internet connection.

Thus, as a citizen of modernity: at the computer table in my sister's rented home in the hills of Laguna Beach, the power of a cable modem inspired my teenage self to work a little in order to create a videogame website that wasn't sustainable and couldn't compete with the impressive professional-seeming videogame websites being made by college graduates—mine was a teenage dream I dreamed aloud, which felt awesome.

A few years later, owing to my shifting interests evolving, my internet music friends replaced my internet videogame friends. In my late teens I preferred emotional music that other people in my school didn't prefer, though plenty of people on the internet had similar preferences.

Then a few years later, my internet music friends were replaced by my internet movie friends.

It is being noted: although my primary interests transitioned from videogames to music to movies, the internet was with me the whole while. And I could always find more people who shared my interests on the internet than in my local community. In my normal daily life it was a goddamn miracle if I found a single person who shared my interests, but on the internet I could find message boards full of people who shared my interests.

Duh: available on my phone these days, the internet is always with me; and movies are still a central interest of mine, but now also books. And, in fact, books didn't come to me through the internet.

After I moved into a Laguna Niguel, California two-bedroom apartment with my roommate-mother, whom I referred to by her first name, and I was twenty, I attended a community college. In an honors class on English literature I made my first friend who was into contemporary adult literature no one else was telling me about—for example: the writing of Katharine Dunn, Horacio Castellanos Moya, Helen DeWitt—and his readerly devotion profoundly realigned my own perspective, facing my thoughts toward enormous possibilities previously unknown to me.

Okay, the initial and rather typical reason for my Southern California relocation: a desire to pen movies. To me, the truth of photography seemed way more accessible than the truth of writing: I felt drawn to the pulse of life in movies, and the beginning of my adult writing focused on screenplays. Though my writing interests now most pertain to the life in books, after having lived in Los Angeles for fifteen years (and two years in Portland, Oregon). The change came to me because the movie world seemed to lack a place for me; not to say that the literary world has a place for me, but I can live in literature through interior resources. I could let go of screenplays, but I could not let go of writing, and I have adapted myself into books for the sake of survival.

A blessing of mine: my current job is relevant to my central interests. I am the producer of a radio show that covers literary fiction and poetry, and my best friends I most often see, my active central friends, are my elderly coworkers: one is the show host, whom Norman Mailer once called this nation's greatest reader, which demonstrates how long he has been the host—I am also the host's personal assistant, which means I shop and perform similar ancillary chores for him; our other coworker-friend is the show editor, who often seems happy despite being more than double my age, which impresses me. A graduate of Yale University, he was once something of a movie executive, a onetime movie director, and a longtime writer of screenplays.

We remote tape the radio show during the pandemic. And on days we tape we also eat together, often outside a neighborhood Italian restaurant. When dining together we tend to fondly recall our past lives as rabbits who lived in the garden of Mr. McGregor.

Less frequently I see my few friends who are closer to my own age, since I do not work with them, and much of our time is bound to burdens of the adult world. It is indeed accurate to say that I am no longer, as it is, close with my generation most interested in comic book movies, tv shows, and podcasts. Which is fine with me, because there is nothing I want less in life than to be a part of my time. Even on the internet I evade rampant conversations about popular topics. Even on the internet I am something of a reclusive oddball eccentric.

Other people are into their things and I'm into mine: my interest in movies remains passionate, and I manifest my passion for books by writing them. I chat about books with my two coworkers who know more about literature than anyone I've previously known, and I speak about movies with my specialized internet friends, plus a few old friends who live in Los Angeles. Though—and you can relate—my book friends aren't the same as my movie friends, and neither group is the same as me; I have more things in common with some people than others, but there is always a little or huge untouched part of me. And this is fine with me because I'm used to it.

Sometimes you hear about the voice of the millions or billions, the masses, and okay, I listen to minor voices of the hundreds and such; they are my people, and I am one of them.

My target audience as a writer, my demographic, doesn't exist as far as I know.

My poetry book before this book, *The Mystery of Everything Everywhere,* was self-published through Neon Burrito Publishing, like this book.

Neon Burrito Publishing is a company I started with my old friend Morgan, who was and still is a writer, although now he is less into writing than I am. The company name came from him, and we first published three poetry books we cowrote: *Frank Zappa & Barry Manilow*, *the name of this book is untitled but that's a bit of a lie*, and *Eudaimonia*.

Morgan and I wrote our poems before thinking about publishing them, just for ourselves, and they each represent a different year of our lives. After we published them we combined them into *Basic Mutant Psychosis: Annals of Los Angeles 2014-2016*. Then in 2017 we published a similar poetry book, *Baker's Dozen*, followed by Morgan pausing from writing for three years, until Morgan returned with ten poems in *The Mystery of Everything Everywhere*.

My friend Alessandra and I first cowrote a poetry book published by Neon Burrito, *Everything Within*, and ten of her poems are in *The Mystery of Everything Everywhere*, too. Clearly, Alessandra and I are fascinated by everything.

My self-published books not yet mentioned:

1. My first novella, *Larry Angeles*, autofiction written in everyman prose
2. The wackiest thing I've ever made, my own pinnacle of weirdness, *My Autobiography Is My Manifesto: Volume One*, a book with the dimensions of a magazine and the interior design of a caveman, there was also a less wacky but still wacky version published with the dimensions of a normal book, *automanifest*—my life story from its beginning to age twenty, intended to feel like an adult-children's book
3. A book of short stories cowritten with Morgan, *Cosmic Robotics,* which has some autofiction of mine but also a fictive story that begins with teleportation
4. *Oscar Wilde's The Picture of Dorian Gray*, collected prose, with one section about creating the book
5. Interior reflection categorized as essays, *Stormy Fortune*

All published through so-called Neon Burrito Publishing. Though I didn't publish the three books I wrote between *Stormy Fortune* and *The Mystery of Everything Everywhere*. You see: I was wanting a publisher to want me, but I couldn't find one. It seems as if I don't belong anywhere except where I am, and I have to accept this: a common topic in my writing, already crystal-clear in this book at this point.

My three unpublished books:

1. *Sometimes I Die, Sometimes I Find Myself,* which includes the true story of when I was stabbed, the true story of me walking around my neighborhood, and the true story of me ordering adult movies for the first time
2. *Who has the keys,* a two-parter: one, a record of an impossible long-distance relationship, and two, a version of me who never stopped writing screenplays; the book ends with a description of my concept for the screenplay of a cannibal love story
3. A fictionalized account of a me who never left Ohio, *Gem City,* the same me but in Ohio

The title of the last feature-length screenplay I wrote: *Gem City.* That's right: after I switched my writing from screenplays to books, a screenplay about an imagined writer transformed into a book about me as a writer. And this is another difference, for me, between books and movies: I'd write screenplays for anticipated actors (the *Gem City* screenplay was about a female), while in a book I can play the lead. I can't act on camera but I can act in paragraphs, and I don't know the inside of anyone else as well as I know the inside of me. I am—I really am—open to writing about topics besides myself, but I keep writing about myself, and I refer to this as The Shawn Michael Sullivan Literary Universe.

So far, a few of my family members and friends have read my books. I must confess that things have not gone smoothly. No, my private writing life has not been impeccable. And my professional writing life doesn't exist. Yet still I keep writing, writing, which indicates that I find loneliness resourceful. Yes: writing frees me from the confines of life. Yes: my worrisome aspects prompt my own laughter, since everything terrible is obvious. This is existential dumpster diving under a full moon for kicks.

I'm trusting my instincts while sharing myself through words, that's my writing style, and above all else I devote my personal time and attention toward reading and writing books, watching movies, and walking around my neighborhood alone: nothing affects me for the better as regularly and intimately as these things, such that my memories of reading a favorite book and watching a favorite movie are in the same memory bank as my favorite days in general—life's rewards arrive to me through both life and art; personal taste.

The same as others before me, I write to make sense of my experience in the world, partly because writing is free, therapy costs money, and my family and friends can't relate. In some ways that is funny. Sad in other ways. Depending on how you look at it. And I accept this risk I take, as I would rather exist as funny or sad than not exist at all. I am both courageous and foolish, and I am one because I am the other. This writing is the me that I am confessing, like Saint Augustine's *Confessions*: days lived as pages written.

My being a writer is my idea, fully supported by my inner child. If one must, one does.

Scrumptious data: this section of the book is being written while I am reading *The Prophets*, by Robert Jones, Jr. And similar to how I don't often find internet-type friends in my community, I don't often find literary writing on the internet.

The Prophets is the variety of book that elevates my perspective on the possibilities of writing. I cherish its spectrum of philosophy, its emotional density, the scope of its vision, and the tone of its perspective. It is about slaves named Samual and Isaiah. They live on a Mississippi plantation named Empty, and they sleep in a barn they tend to. They tend to each other too.

Brooding Samuel is probably hotter than cheerful Isaiah, although Isaiah is nicer. You know this because of how young and innocent Puah thinks of Samuel, and how lesbian and wise Sarah thinks of Isaiah. I admire this fully composed reality. Reading this kind of well-written book engulfs my own senses, delightfully overwhelming me. I keep experiencing hot Mississippi weather. Hot even under the shade of a tree.

Greatly admiring this book that should be talked about, I'll further recommend its author to the show host. We prefer to cover books that should be talked about. And I prefer this kind of reading.

Reading *The Prophets* while writing this book makes this book better, there's no doubt about that to me. Every book I read becomes part of what I write, so reading a good book is always a good influence.

If there were a bibliography of the books and movies mentioned in my writing, I would be proud of it. It's a longish list now. And it keeps transpiring inside my writing that comes from my life. Reading is part of my life. Mentioning: I would not feel as in control of the philosophical shape of these paragraphs if not for my contemporaneous reading of *The Prophets*.

Would I have decided to read *The Prophets* if I didn't have my job?

What will my life lead me to when the show host retires?

What does my future look like from a general perspective?

Is this the beginning, middle, or end of my opportunity to partake in outsider writing?

If all I've so-far written will be all I ever write, what does that mean in terms of who I became as a writer?

I became whatever this is.

This book is my inevitability.

The people who want me to concentrate on building narratives are going to be so pissed. Here I go building myself again.

Probably my favorite part about being me is sleep.

And when I write books I try to be both outright honest and as outrageous as I can be. At the end of the first draft of *Gem City* the dead protagonist lived on the moon with his grandmother. Which ending was changed, sadly. I did keep the scene about ghosts on boats in a cemetery pond. What I wanted from the moon: a light scene about missing my grandmother and wanting to die. The final draft of *Who has the keys* ends with the plot synopsis of a screenplay I wrote (both in life and in the book), concerning a spiritual connection between a female cannibal and a man who longs to be eaten. Some of my friends deemed that ending ridiculous and sophomoric, and I had put all of myself into it, really believed in it. Suddenly, a spontaneous but thematically equivalent side story: in my past, when I was twenty-five, I shared the screenplay to my cannibal love story, *Adrina, You Swallow Me,* with two dear friends. And the first friend didn't know how to respond. He didn't know how to put into words how little he got out of it. A wordless disappointment. The second friend had a positive attitude regarding the general product. The second friend considered it a noble creative endeavor with some memorable moments. But it was the first friend's response that lingered in my mind. I felt so bummed I moved from Los Angeles to Portland for two years. At any rate, the beginning of my last book of unpublished prose, *Sometimes I Die, Sometimes I Find Myself,* features a fairy granting the protagonist a wish, and the protagonist, who is inspired by the true story of me, wishes for his roommate to leave their apartment for a little bit of time, and the ending of that book highlights the time in which my creative interests first encountered The Golden Age of Porn (which will be further discussed just ahead). One may say that my outrageous side gets me in trouble, but I consider a little trouble good for us.

Anyone who doesn't give all of themselves to what they do should reconsider what they do.

But though I live to write, my writing style is not the same as my lifestyle: as in, in theory I live in these words, but in actuality I experience the mechanics of the real world like a typical human. Because here we are, genuinely baked with star ingredients, and still we age, our body changes, and my hair is moving from my scalp to my nose and ears. Some weight is new to me, must be my metabolism. Is healthy eating ahead of me? Pilates soon? Daily pills eventually? In terms of ample facial moisturizer, is this the perfect time for that, or was the perfect time a decade ago? How far behind my future am I? And I grind my teeth while I sleep and I am mortal, etcetera and whatnot.

Many friends, family members, and people who know me would say that I am being beyond outrageous in terms of my interest in The Golden Age of Porn.

Pornography from the perspective of theatrical movies, pornography as an art form, is fresh to me, and thus stimulates my sense of creative possibilities, though most everyone I know would prefer for me to stimulate my interests elsewhere. In fact, I have never before begun to like a thing that is so doubtlessly shunned by so many. I am telling you: these old films are no longer masturbation material, first of all. And though there's copious sex, there's more than sex. In this circumstance people are more prone to believe in their fears than believe in me. Thus it fits in perfectly with my common interests.

My reaction to the movie *Blue Money* (1971):

It's not pornography, it's a movie about making pornography on the cusp of Nixon's reelection, and of course Nixon is trying to shut down the adult movie business, sounds just like Nixon. This is the story of a hot af French Quebecian who just wants to score big loads of money, finish building his boat, and leave everything behind him. But the government won't let him. Because the government is seriously rude. He's a father and his baby momma's own perspective is a side story. This hot af French Quebecian with gorgeous pouty lips is also the director, it's his story, and this whole movie is about him.

It's so good. The distributor compared it to Cassevetes but nah. It's Jacques Demy's *Model Shop* but about porn instead of depression.

My reaction to the movie *Bat Pussy* (~1970):

You know, not so outrageously, I had expected a pornographic parody of *Batman*. But this is something else entirely. Really its own kind of thing. The central characters are the married couple Buddy and Sam. The vast majority of this movie takes place in their apartment, in what is speculated to be Arkansas, based on Buddy's ass tattoo. In the beginning Buddy reads *Screw* magazine while Sam is on the bed, then Buddy joins Sam on the bed, and the bulk of the movie is their conversations on the bed, amid sexual behavior but no sex at all. In the final section Bat Pussy joins them, to interrupt their smut making—inspired by *Screw* magazine, Buddy has taken out a camera—but Buddy overtakes Bat Pussy, and she becomes part of the smut. Buddy calls her Bat Woman a few times, which Sam once corrects. Bat Pussy coughs a couple times. Sam takes out a dildo. Sometimes the sound cuts out for a brief moment, a couple times Buddy looks toward the production crew, direction is being given.

The fact that you can watch this, that it exists, feels astonishing. It is speculated to have been made back when theaters made their own movies, though no one is certain who made it, or why or when it was made.

My reaction to the movie *Matinee Idol* (1984):

Going from early Joseph W. Sarno to Alain Patrick's *Blue Money* to Henri Pachard's *Matinee Idol* is witnessing a lot of change. A massive development in cinematic pornography.

Everything Alain Patrick dreams of in *Blue Money* is actualized by the time of *Matinee Idol*, which is a Hollywood insider movie about the porn industry. *Matinee Idol* begins on a movie set and ends in a production office, with two producers looking at the camera and asking you (the viewer) if you're the pretty-faced big-dick star of the future: a Hollywood dream through a pornographic lens.

I can't put into words the lightness of *Matinee Idol*, except by using the word lightness to describe the movie, so I just did my best there. It's very much a Peter Bogdanovich porn movie. It understands the life and reality of actors, and it portrays their burdens they surmount through grace and good humor. It is simply true that there is a sex scene involving toes, and that it's an intentionally funny scene. Traditional sex scenes occur while actors play their roles, which we know because we see the production crew and the production meetings. We witness the production of pornography, are given insider knowledge, hear the conversations that take place between scenes, and of course there is a production we don't see, the production of this production, and it's so well accomplished. *Matinee Idol* is rather expertly crafted and thoroughly enjoyable.

The Golden Age of Pornography isn't my everything, it will never complete me, and I don't offer it all of me—it's fair to say I don't need it—though it's also fair to say that watching pornography assists my familiarity with the creative possibilities of cinematic pornography, which I can't miss out on, personally. I want to be wherever and however art is.

I've dated people who tell me they understand art better than I do. I say to them, Okay.

My life is my art, and I barely understand my life. Accurate.

My art is my life I write about, and I consider my writing its best when I really crack myself open, in terms of the capabilities of words as portals into people. I dive fully inside myself to get to the bottom of me, because life is a complex number of simplicities. They say that strength means how much truth you can bear, Robert Jones, Jr. wrote in *The Prophets*, and this is a note to self: lots of my worries seem true to me, but sometimes the truth I bear is only a worry.

Something else is on my mind right now and for a while. A different mood for a number of pages.

A specific plan over the weekend: drive a mile across Melrose Avenue to visit my old friend I've known since Ohio. Because he invited me over and I said yes. He lives next to Pink's Hot Dogs and we see each other about once a month.

Here I am inside my friend's apartment. He says hello and I too say hello.

My old friend sits across from me while he rolls a joint and I play a videogame he tells me about. Since I no longer purchase videogames, visiting my old friend allows me to catch up on what is happening in the world of videogames.

Cool.

This old friend is a recurring character in my books.

I feel lucky that he hasn't moved away from Los Angeles, which he sometimes speaks of doing.

Because of how expensive this city is.

Because many people here have more money and success than he does.

And because if he returned to Ohio he would feel like a normal person in a positive way.

In Ohio you can just live, while here they ask you to always be working at life.

Life *is* work!

This dream city can make the mistake of thinking of normalcy as negligence, while it takes all our concentration for my old friend and I to behave normally.

My friend and I have talked about this before, and many other things, anything.

It is true that he moved to Southern California for the same reason I did: movies.

We moved here with a dream: yes.

Our dream was to become creative professionals, people paid to make movies, which is different from the life we now lead.

But if your dream rejects you, don't reject life: we are working on developing this mindset.

Again and always: everything terrible is obvious, but more than the terrible exists.

When my old friend and I are together we're glad to be ourselves, so it calms us. He understands that I understand and vice versa. Today I tell him, Yeah, just been writing this book (that you're currently reading). Talking about my writing is a way of talking about myself as an object. My old friend listens. He has followed my life narrative. He has witnessed narrative arcs. And too we have shared significant moments together: he has been a part of my life narrative.

This story of my friend and I, is it part of this narrative or too light? Filler or killer, meaningless or meaningful?

My friend is a person in my community who collects more movies than I do. I'm lucky to know him. We start the evening by smoking pot, chatting, playing videogames, and listening to music. Then the movie begins: *Outside the Law*, directed by Tod Browning, starring Priscilla Dean and Lon Chaney. How fortunate I am to have a friend who would buy this movie, and watch it with me. How glad I feel to be alive while *Outside the Law* plays.

We're Tod Browning stans.

The same meal my old friend and I ate in *Gem City*: after the movie my old friend makes us buttered grilled cheese sandwiches. And we drink Capri Sun. I feel so, so, so alive. This is meaningful nothing special. For dessert, we eat Fruit Gushers he happened to have on hand. I tell him I want to write a book that feels like a movie. I tell him I want to write a book that takes an hour and a half to read. I tell him I want to write a book that gives more than it takes. He nods. He likes the sound of that. And we're listening to music while smoking another joint. And I'm holding a videogame control, playing the *Super Mario 3D All-Stars* version of *Super Mario 64* (my all-time favorite videogame).

My old friend says he better leave to pick up his girlfriend from work. Then he says goodbye and I too say goodbye.

Palate cleanser.

Here I am on a sidewalk, traveling between my apartment and a restaurant.

Traveling is the primary purpose of a sidewalk, and I like using a sidewalk for its primary purpose.

Sometimes I might fuck up in life, but not on sidewalks.

You know, I have heard it said that I possess a distinguishing gait.

As in, I walk funny.

I don't even possess the gait of a normal person: my god.

Oh well.

I walk funny and I point my feet inward when I'm standing still. I stand pigeon toed but that information is tangential to the fact that I am walking on a sidewalk like you are supposed to.

I can do this.

I am doing this.

I do this all the time.

This stretch of sidewalk between my apartment building and The Original Farmers Market is as familiar to me as the freckles on my face.

And I like walking here as much as I like seeing dolphins break water surface.

CBS Television City is beside me.

How many people have visited here to be an audience member on *The Price Is Right*?

More than twenty.

A couple times some years ago, since it is right here, and is free, I was an audience member for a taping of *The Late Late Show with Craig Ferguson*.

Craig Ferguson doesn't even host the show anymore.

Whatever.

Lena Dunham was the guest.

Okay.

The sun is above me.

So often the sun is above me in Los Angeles.

A little too often.

There is a little too much sunlight, in my opinion.

I think sunlight is overrated.

Sunlight is mad hyped but it isn't my vibe.

I'm a night person.

A nighthawk.

I'm a bandit who steals life from time at night.

Fuck sunlight.

Seriously.

But I can't change that. And it's a lot of wasted energy to be mad at something you can't change.

You're okay sunlight.

You're not for me but you're okay.

Fuck you and best wishes.

I wish the world spun so slowly the night lasted for days in Los Angeles.

Like in Alaska.

It's not scientifically possible here?

Science can be a major buzzkill.

I like the science of possibility.

I wish it were possible for nights to last a month, like in Alaska, but in Los Angeles, with this weather.

Sometimes changing reality isn't as easy as making wishes.

Sometimes reality is as easy as making wishes, though, so I always think it's worth trying.

That's my opinion, but what do I know, except that I can walk on a sidewalk.

I am perambulating.

I am now a peripatetic individual on a sidewalk adjacent to a parking lot.

And my destination is approaching.

My arrival is imminent.

I am achieving the goal of walking from one place to another.

This is a capability of mine.

And now I am here, at the place where I should be.

I have received a text about the situation: I am aware that the people I am meeting are already at this franchise Italian restaurant where my family and I regularly eat.

Classify our tradition as mostly random and semi-circumstantial. We do this because we can and we do.

What we do: when someone in my family visits me, we eat at this franchise Italian restaurant, which is headquartered in Dallas, Texas. What. Sure.

I am walking across the dining room, and I like the feeling of this place.

Its center is tables covered in white cloth, with booths around the wall.

My family is on the far side of the room.

I see them.

Frank Sinatra is playing.

Frank Sinatra always plays here.

There are black-and-white photos on the wall.

The past is celebrated here.

The past is the present in this franchise Italian restaurant, and now I am at the table, greeting my mother, her sister, and her sister's son.

I am being visited by my mother, an aunt, and a cousin.

My mother lives with this sister.

My cousin lives in his own house but in the same area.

An area outside of Phoenix, Arizona.

People live in the goddamn desert.

I am glad they are visiting me.

I sit at the booth.

Menus are being read.

Decisions are being made.

Meal related things are transpiring here at this booth.

Realistic.

I decide to order what I often order: a dish that comes with a free dish. I eat one dish and take the other home. That, indeed, is a special offer. And my routine selection.

It is the end of November in the year before the plague, Thanksgiving has just passed, and the biggest thing happening in my life is I am about to fly to New Zealand for the end of a relationship.

Topics are being discussed over conversations with my family members.

My aunt speaks about running her coffee truck. I say she is a valuable member of her community because she runs her coffee truck. I mean it when I say it. She thanks me. I hope she knows I'm not being polite but honest: this is how I think of her doing that.

My mother has five siblings and this sister is the youngest. She's in her late fifties now. My mother loves all of her siblings but she is closer to some of them, and I appreciate all of my cousins but I am closer to some of them. My mother is close with this sister, they currently live together, and specifically my mother lives in this sister's house.

My mother has not owned a home since days long gone, back in Ohio. She last owned a home she had built after her dating service franchise business boomed in the year her father died (which financial success she considered her father's blessing).

Though the times changed and left my mother behind.

The internet overtook her business demographic, and she sold the house on the hill, years after a divorce. She doesn't own a home any longer, and she lives with her sister outside of Phoenix, Arizona.

In the fucking desert.

Jesus Christ. The sunlight there: I don't want to talk about it. I don't want to think about it.

My mother is close to this sister and I am close to this aunt who used to live outside of Chicago, Illinois. When I was younger we would travel from outside of Dayton, Ohio, to visit this family outside of Chicago. We would drive. That was chill. I liked doing that. And I was close with this cousin of mine.

In the time of my youth, before the internet, I thought that getting along with people was something you did in person. I got along with the people around me instead of the people in the cloud: life used to be like that, before the internet, and it can still be like that, although such life exists on the internet now, too. Common knowledge. But anyway back when I was younger I was friends with this cousin and now we're not close, because we don't any longer share significant interests. When younger it was videogames. Other family members didn't play videogames as much as I did, but he did, which provided us with a special bond: united by our affection for videogames.

I don't know if he still plays videogames but I know I don't. And now he works in banking, and he is into sports and cars, which are guy interests I don't have. Not to be hard on banking, sports or cars, they are just not my thing. And literature and cinema are not my cousin's thing.

We're still family but our dynamic has shifted over the years, so we don't have much to talk about—our familiarity with each other disappeared like the dodo.

Oh no.

Oh yes: and there he is, my cousin I can still relate to in a theoretical sense. Because I know that he too wants his life to be a little different than it is. He too wants to be someone he is not, I am aware, because my mother tells me about his relatable tribulations. Though he has different tribulations than I do, and he solves them differently than I do—we have almost nothing in common except family blood—still I understand him in a theoretical sense, though I do not know what the hell to say to him today or any day these days.

We can't even discuss how sad life is, because we don't even think of life as sad in a similar manner. To better understand ourselves: he drives cars, I read books. That is a significant difference. A chasm between us. Any child able to talk could tell you that cars and books are different.

I can't mention these topics in conversation with my family right now. I can't bring up these topics this way and expect these people, my family, to consider the conversation worthwhile. These are whispers I share with you the reader.

After our meal, my family members and I walk up Fairfax Avenue as a group. My family walks to their nearby franchise hotel, and I carry my take-home dish.

My apartment building is a block North at the corner of Fairfax and Beverly, while their hotel is three blocks East, so our paths cross at this point; I say goodbye to my mother and aunt, though my cousin has walked ahead of us. My cousin has broken apart from the group. No goodbye to or from him. I appreciate his style.

I see them again the next morning.

They are about to head back, and I invited them to a deli behind my apartment building.

I walk in and they are at a booth against the wall. Everyone orders breakfast.

We delight in each other's company.

I am not able to chat about my favorite books, movies or music with them, but that is fine. They feel the same about me. And they respect me for who I am, same as I do them: family.

After breakfast they're leaving.

We're outside now.

My cousin has purchased a bag of pastries because he ate one and said, "Now I understand why this place is famous."

I didn't know this place was famous. How convenient.

My cousin says I should visit Phoenix.

I think that sounds crazy.

I heard that the night before he went out without my mother or his mother, and he drank alone at a nearby bar.

He had never contacted me, but I understood why.

He thought it was better to be at the bar alone than be at the bar with me.

Happens.

Relatable.

There is no way I'll visit him in Phoenix, and I barely know what I can say to him about anything.

He says I have his phone number, and also he says he is thinking about giving up on phones. He says we think about our phones too much. I hear he's experiencing relationship trouble.

I am hugging them and they are leaving and is this a side story or part of the main story.

This is atmosphere.

This is mood.

At this point I want to be finished writing this book, because I feel as if I've successfully established the voice and perspective of this book, and I like short books, but I know, and it's true, that you have to put in extra effort for the sake of deeper rewards. I'm feeling emotional after writing the previous chapters but no, this book isn't near done: only beginning.

Volume One of *My Autobiography Is My Manifesto* ended when I was twenty, and this book, *Volume Two*, picks up when I'm thirty-seven. What about the years between? Well, every book I've written since *Larry Angeles* has been a product of the year in which it was written, so my life story has been illustrated back to when I was thirty-two. So what about the years between twenty and thirty-two? Hm, maybe this series is non-chronological, or maybe I'll never write about those years: a slight mystery. On a future day I might write of that me in some way I'm just not thinking of today, but probably not, and let us get into why: writing about my childhood in *Volume One* felt easy, but complexities bloom after I become an adult. Complexities like shifts within my reality. Now that I do not live in Portland, and now that it is close to a decade since I did, I am not certain that I could write of living in Portland with the emotional exactitude that I prefer as a reader and writer. Even further back are the years I spent working at Costco, and to recall those days as they were, to compose a narrative portrait of me in a time when my life was slipping away from my dreams, could I live that again and would I want to, or listen, imagine this: how could I write of the beginning and end of my longest relationship when that person is now married with two kids? Wow: her husband and kids would hate me. The story of when I moved back to Los Angeles: I'm not sure I can capture all those intricacies as my present self, because a lot of what made sense to me then no longer does. This is one reason why I feel a need to keep writing about my life as it happens. To make the record possible.

What I can say is I definitely participate in the universe, and my books are writerly duplicates of years in my life. I may repeat the perspective but I don't repeat the years; I may say the same thing thrice, but I cannot live the same day twice.

Popsicles.

At the end of the year of the pandemic, in December, I am at my friend's at 7am, because I told him I would be. This early since I want him to know that I mean business about a short movie I've pitched to him. I learn my friend had COVID but is over it. I choose not to dwell on this topic because we're enjoying seeing each other and we want to make this short movie. He says he wants to go to a coffee place so we go to a coffee place. He asks if I want coffee but I don't. He chit-chats with the guy behind the counter. I think he's friends with a guy who works at a coffee shop. After we leave I learn that that guy is the owner, and my friend learned his neighborhood coffee shop owner is also a model, after seeing him on a billboard in Tokyo. I ask about the trip to Tokyo. I hear a bit about the trip to Tokyo. I learn the coffee shop owner who is also a model on a Tokyo billboard is also a cameraperson in the movie industry. My friend is a cameraperson in the movie industry, too. I met this friend after I moved to California when I was twenty. We shared formative years dreaming of movies, and off and on I still dream of movies. After I finished writing *Sometimes I Die, Sometimes I Find Myself,* I was sitting around wondering what else there is in life besides writing books, and I started dreaming about a movie. I used to make movies with this friend, back when I made movies. Back when I thought of movies as my future. I asked my friend if he wanted to get the band back together, and he did! This friend is such a professional movie person his camera career paid for his house in Echo Park, and the house he built in Joshua Tree, too. He genuinely built a house in Joshua Tree, with a cameraperson friend of his. Built a house. In Joshua Tree. Sometimes I buy myself a king-size Snicker bar to experience thrills. I pitched my friend an idea about a city opera. I mentioned *Man with a Movie Camera* and said we wouldn't need actors. I am obsessed with the fact that in early movie history, when modernity was modern, and cities were newish, movies were made to celebrate cities; cities felt so big they needed movies, and movies felt so big they needed cities. I pitched him the idea of a short movie titled *Tomorrow, Yesterday, and Today are on the Same Timeline*, and with Los Angeles locations as lead characters. I want to portray Los Angeles as a city of the future, past, and present, and when I tell him about this he becomes excited, which makes me more excited. I propose the idea of a movie timeframe stretching from sunrise to sunset, and a trip from Venice Beach to Santa Monica to Westwood to West Hollywood to Miracle Mile to Crenshaw to South LA to Watts Towers to East LA to Downtown to Echo Park to Little Bangladesh. He is into this and I am into his being into this. This morning we are headed to East LA. It is called pre-production. Location scouting. The proposed runtime for this short is six minutes. It's a travelogue in some ways. We have the address for Our Lady of Solitude, a church that opened its door on Christmas Day in 1925. That's my idea for what we could shoot in East LA. On our way there we eat indica edibles, which I brought along. We arrive at the church and it isn't much from the outside. And we can't go in. So we walk up and down the street, absorbing the environment and imagining our short movie. It feels good. I feel fortunate to have this friend. I feel blessed to have this day. We're driving away and my friend is noticing things we pass. I had only planned to visit the church, but my friend senses that we're not finished. There's more looking around to do. He notices a cemetery from the freeway, and he asks if we can stop at the cemetery. So we stop at the cemetery. It's a big ol' cemetery and we're speaking about what we'll shoot the short on. If we'll use film or not. We decide it won't be film but digital. Because we're not yet sure of all we'll shoot. This cemetery is cool. We talk about shooting in this cemetery. My friend tells a story about cemeteries being tricky to shoot in. One time a guard ran across a cemetery to yell at him. Then we drive to Watts Towers and I have never been to Watts Towers but I know it by reputation, and I pictured it while picturing a short movie that celebrates LA. We arrive at Watts Towers and it's closed off for renovation. The renovation has been slowed down by the onslaught of the plague. My friend and I dream of living in one of the houses next to Watts Towers. How cool it would be to wake up with Watts Towers in front of you. Then instead of driving on the freeway from Watts Towers back North, we drive on the streets. We are location scouting from the car. Surveying the land. Spending our morning driving up Los Angeles. This is living my best life. This is enough for me. This is all I need. This is fine. This will do. My friend says he fucks with King Taco. He asks if we can stop at a King Taco. We stop at a King Taco. I order a burrito and an horchata. Since interior dining is still not allowed, we eat in my car. Then we drive further up the city taking pictures. We arrive in Downtown and my friend knows of an art bookstore we go to. My friend is a good person so he's searching for a holiday present for his girlfriend's sister, who is into architecture. I am overwhelmed by the number of books in the bookstore. So many books. I want all of them. I can't think of one to buy. Just looking around. Just having a good time. My friend knows how to have a good time. I mainly read books and watch movies about having a good time, so when I do it myself it is like, wow. Again: is this outside the narrative or part of the narrative? Well, in all honesty there is no narrative: it's all me. Will my friend and I end up making this short? What about the rest of the band members, such as the would-be editor who doesn't speak with me any longer? We're driving through Downtown now, and we agree that Downtown offers ample photographic opportunity. There is much in Downtown to put on camera. My friend says he has a building in mind that he wants to check out, so I drive there and we check it out. It's an old building and it's cool.

I know.

Or, I don't know, but I can imagine.

These friends of mine married in December and I'm at their apartment in January. My old friend who lives near Pink's Hot Dogs is present, and his girlfriend, too. I am the fifth wheel, the spare wheel. Well, one should have a spare wheel. I like my friends' significant others because they like each other. I approve of these relationships. Tonight we order hamburgers and watch *The Last American Virgin* together. The movie is the ladies' pick. I want the ladies to pick the movie because then the ladies are on the movie's side. I'm open to any movie so I want the ladies to pick the movie. My old friend had brought along *The Last American Virgin*, and we all end up liking it. The movie watching goes well. And through the night there isn't a fight. There isn't a disagreement. The friends whose apartment this is speak about driving up North in search of a home to buy. Earlier today they visited a home for sale, and they refer to its marketing photos as catfishing. I am riveted by the story of their home shopping endeavor in California country. Morgan will write a poem about this. (I am in the home of the Morgan I mentioned earlier. I could have started this story with Morgan's name but I didn't.) After the conversation Morgan shows us an internet video about a guy who owns lizards. Something from the internet that's interesting. A wholesome night of bonding between friends and we guests leave soon, but I forgot to mention that before the movie we watched vintage cartoons I had brought along: *Cartoon Roots: Halloween Haunts*. The earliest cartoon: 1907. The latest: 1936. While the earliest was on the screen I mentioned how old it is. Morgan made a joke about how he was watching a perfectly fine cartoon that I qualified as old, and, the way he said it, everyone laughed, including me, so I suggested that Morgan should become a stand-up comedian. No sarcasm. We watched *Alice's Mysterious Mystery*, and that felt wild. Walt Disney in 1926. Walt Disney before Mickey Mouse. Old cartoons are my catnip and I watched some with my dear friends who feel roughly the same about life as I do.

For serious.

The revelations that arrive to me through writing about myself are alluring to me at the time of writing, but the book feels fuller when the writing involves other people. The inclusion of other people makes the book larger than me—you know, there's that ultra-famous Walt Whitman line, "I am large, I contain multitudes," and I do contain multitudes like most people, but the multitudinous really accentuates itself within a group setting.

What is infinity times infinity.

My closest internet movie friends consider Paul Thomas Anderson the greatest living film director, and I don't agree with them, but they are my friends. PTA begins shooting a new movie in the year of the pandemic, and they become aware of the initial production location, a gas station, which they visit. Bradley Cooper is present; Alana Haim, too—easily recognizable. Though my internet movie friends identify the young star on their own: the son of Philip Seymour Hoffman, first-time actor Cooper Hoffman. Understandably, they are touched by this casting decision. A lot of what PTA does touches them—although they feel lukewarm about his first movie, *Hard Eight*, which they call *Sydney*, and *Inherent Vice* stirs minor controversy—overall they worship this guy. They experience incandescent feelings regarding the production of his new movie, *Soggy Bottom*. One of them is a recent East coast transplant, and he feels ecstatic. I am delighted by their delight. A gentleman beyond employment shares the majority of information from the first set visit, and his information instantly spreads across the internet, which results in the installation of a private section in the movie message board we all visit (in order to provide the gentleman beyond employment a safe place to share insider information). He begins to daily visit the shooting locations, and I encourage his behavior. It excites me. What the hell else is going on during the pandemic (not a damn thing). I propose that Neon Burrito will publish his diary entries from his set visits. I propose the title *A Diary of Visits to Paul Thomas Anderson Shooting Locations,* which is a reference to *Diary of a Madman*, as only Gogol could have written this particular character. His heart is so pure and I support him even when people start asking questions about him. I tell him to keep going when some in the production crew consider him too unusual to trust. They don't understand what I understand: everything is fine. He is innocent. I want to publish his diary entries for three reasons: one, so he can have his writing published, two, because there is a demographic for this type of information, based on Paul Thomas Anderson's reputation, and three, to troll that demographic. I don't consider any of this serious, and I expect no one to be harmed. Then I am stabbed and I am in the hospital for a while. Then I leave the hospital and check in on things: the gentleman beyond employment is still visiting the production that is still going. Excellent. I tell my significant other about this. She is taking care of me while I am healing from the stabbing. She doesn't consider visiting a message board healthy behavior. She thinks I should pay more attention to the world around me. Later, we break up. I appreciate how she took care of me during my recovery. Then I am slipping away from my internet movie friends, which sometimes happens. Although we share an interest in movies, sometimes our interest gazes in disparate directions. That slipping away from each other can frustrate me, and I can step away from them. Happens. Strong differences in opinion. My prior internet videogame friends, and internet music friends, could tell their own stories. But I left them behind forever, and I return to my internet movie friends. So I return to them and discover that the gentleman beyond employment has continued his mission. But the enterprise has taken on a more serious tone than I anticipated. My proposal was to publish it immediately, but there is vehement opposition against this. They truly consider this information sacred secrets for their privilege alone. I mention that all a reader will be able to do is read about what little the gentleman beyond employment could see, so in fact a reader will dream of the movie with him, and I mention diminishing interest, saying the book should be published during peak interest, for not just the diehard fans, but all curious people. They are resolute about it not being publishable until after the movie's release. I tell them we will have a group discussion about it when the production concludes. The production keeps going and the gentleman beyond employment keeps visiting. Then by chance I stumble upon a past post of his, in which he daydreams of submitting his diary to the production for publication, and I realize that we are far from being on the same page about this. It dawns on me that our dreams lack synchronization, and none of what I thought might happen will.

Although 2020 was the year of the plague, it was also the year of fatigue. In the beginning I felt fear and anger, and then I felt fatigue. I would overcome the fatigue when and how I could.

My internet movie friends and I go back a number of years—not since the beginning but a number of years. When 2020 began, before the pandemic, after I finished my book *Who has the keys*, during some extra time I allowed myself to dream of writing movies again, and I wrote a screenplay for a member of the movie message board, a man younger than me who shared interests with me and had graduated from the NYU Tisch School of the Arts. I figured if anything means anything in this world it's two people liking Abel Ferrara. I sent him a screenplay under ten pages long, titled *The Universe is a Water Person*. The story concerns a man made fun of first by a close friend, next by random strangers at a bar. This man then walks along the ocean shore alone but for his misery, and he chances upon a stranded individual. This stranded individual happens to be a sea creature, although the protagonist never knows this. The man revives the sea creatures who jumps back into the ocean. I categorized the potential script production as a pipe dream. The member of the movie message board was warm and receptive. Days passed. I stopped visiting the message board around the time the pandemic began. I returned to the message board and the member with my screenplay was there. This online movie community was part of his daily routine. Sweet. Glad to know him. The pandemic had begun so I didn't even ask him if he had shot the script. I knew it wouldn't have been possible and so I wrote him another script that seemed more possible: *Everything is Fucked and There's Still Monday*. In this script everyone wears a mask. It's a party of friends and the friends are werewolves, a sea creature, a vampire, a warlock and two witches. He thanked me for the script. Days passed. The pandemic persisted and that was a major fucking drag. What the shit. I wrote him another script about one person, under ten pages like all of them, this one titled *It's Yesterday Again*. It was about the monotony of our days in the plague: one guy sitting around doing a bunch of nothing, sometimes texting, sometimes chatting with his internet friends. I called every script a pipe dream and none of them ended up being made as the pandemic continued. So little was possible in those days. Had we missed out on supreme opportunities or were they future possibilities? Were the scripts even good in the first place?

The internet reminded me about the experience of creative failures during the pandemic. Nothing in my life was anything going well; my life didn't feel under my control. Agency schmagency: things didn't become any better when it was up to only me. Fatalism felt like realism and I kept fighting to stay at the same place in life: why? Because I did. Because I do. I must belong where I am, or at least I keep staying here, and at this point in the writing of this book it's a near month after my thirty-fucking-seventh birthday, toward the beginning of the second year of the pandemic, and by now Richard Brautigan's *The Abortion: An Historical Romance 1966* sits next to me. I'm on page sixty-nine. It was gifted to me by a woman I will visit tonight: she and I get along with each other, laugh at each other's jokes, and she's interested in watching pornography with me. Blessed. Tonight we're going to watch *Hot and Saucy Pizza Girls*, directed by Bob Chinn. In this adult movie, John Holmes is the manager of a pizza parlor. Pretty cool that she will watch this with me. She is a writer herself. She has read my writing and I have read hers. She appreciates my writing although she doesn't quite know what to do with it, and I appreciate her writing but she doesn't need me. We are each other's emotional support. Tonight she is going to order a fourteen-inch pizza with spinach, sun-dried tomatoes, feta, tomato sauce, and mozzarella; we didn't buy the movie, we're going to stream it for free from xHamster. She lives across Pico over by Landmark Theatres. So I go to her and we watch the movie and eat the pizza, it happens. Then, with time remaining in our movie date night, we follow the first adult movie with a second: *Let My Puppets Come*. This is a puppet movie that's so legitimately pornography we watch it on a porn site, and a real woman strips for a puppet male as part of his fetish: her underwear on his head, she throws grapes at him. That actress never had another job like that again, with a puppet at least. Before sleep, I read the Richard Brautigan book my date gave me; beside me, she reads Joan Didion. Then, lights out. And we wake together in the night. As in I start talking to her while she's sleeping so she wakes up and we spend some time together in the night. Do we want to have sex? We wait for the morning. So then in the morning we have sex and shower together. I propose the idea that we buy a horse we name John Holmes. She asks me what I know about horses. I mention that I grew up in the country. We talk about how she might be moving back to New York City soon. Or rather, she already has an apartment in NYC, and she'll be returning to it soon. Her friend subletting her apartment will be leaving soon. I leave her place early because a parking sign states that I have to move my car before ten. While driving away from her I text her that I'm not yet home and I already miss her. You shouldn't text while driving.

The things I start saying, I mean seriously, they sound so serious: what if—just what if—I could tend to my life as much as I tend to my thoughts and feelings. My mind craves constant stimulation, I write to stimulate myself, and I say I favor peace but I don't seem to know how to live in it. My existence is not a model existence. My perspective is not a universal perspective. My life story is not even the size of a dime in the narrative of this planet. And I feel about my books the way I feel about my life: good on my good days and bad on my bad days. Other people's opinions influence me. And like many other people I listen closest to objections, leaving behind kindness. Everyone who sees the bad sees what the people who see only the good don't see, I conclude, instead of concluding that the people who see only the bad can miss out on the good. When the bad says the good doesn't matter I feel a sense of panic: that's an existential similarity between my perspective on my books and my life. And life is not like this so much as I am.

Sometimes when life doesn't feel right to me, I think life is the problem. Sometimes when I don't feel accepted I think it's because of what people want. Sometimes I think anything is the problem but me. Sometimes I wake up without wanting my day to begin. Sometimes I wonder why I haven't died yet indeed. Sometimes my thoughts are far away from where I wish they were. Sometimes my thoughts hide in dark places, and when I call out to them, trying to draw them back to me, they don't budge. Sometimes how I feel isn't how I want to feel. Sometimes my feelings make their own decisions. Sometimes neither the past nor the future seem to matter. I hope on the day I die I'm in a good mood.

We are on the phone in a traditional style, with our voices, no video, and he is informing me about his current life situation, a year-long relationship that recently ended, "Yeah. It was an abusive relationship. She physically hit me. She punched me outside by my car. We would break up and get back together, because of the sex. We had great sex. She is a mother. She has a daughter. She would spend time on the phone with the father. On our one overseas vacation together, to islands, she spent most of her time on the phone with the father. And we kept going even after the sex felt less rewarding, following the second breakup. But our third breakup was the final ending, and I have bought a house over on Mad River Road. Currently I live in my parent's basement—not the house you knew in our youth, but a bigger house they bought after the kids moved out. I am staying here until I move into my own house. We had spoken about where her daughter's room might be. Now I am past her and I can't u-turn. Many times my family and friends had tried to talk me out of the relationship. No one could understand why I was in the relationship. Yeah, she is a coworker. She still works with me. I still see her in the office, but we don't talk. I don't believe in staying friends. One person is always chasing the other."

When I meet philosophical people whom I get along with because we think about being bothered by the world in a similar manner: that was the guy on the phone and me back in Ohio, when he was in high school and I had graduated a year prior. We thought it was all preposterous: life. Everything. Life is rude. He would visit me and we would talk about life while drinking from my mother's liquor cabinet. Drink and talk about life, with a movie on in the background. My mother was already in Laguna Niguel so I had the Ohio apartment to myself. My mother and I had moved from the house on the hill to an apartment after her initial Matchmaker International location shuttered, and a few years after her divorce from my step-father. She had opened a neighborhood Matchmaker International, but the internet had found the industry. She left for California and the apartment was mine alone back when my friend would come over after his high school classes, and we would do what we most wanted to do: because of the kind of people we were. Stuck in our heads. He's a non-drinker who takes antidepressants these days. And he works for the city: he selects the people to be in juries. He had been a prosecutor after graduating from law school, and back then he told me he was the only pro-criminal prosecutor in the city. The other prosecutors were pro-law. He would aim for the lowest possible punishment. This was during the opioid epidemic.

Two previous friends I don't speak with anymore because they both decided that was best for them: they're both men and it was their decision, never any conversation about it. Ghosted. The things I mention because I feel I have to! Easily imagine: the other person won't even listen.

A pandemic quarantine arrived first, then a curfew following the Black Lives Matter protests, and although so much about those days was so heavy, in those nights I would drink beer while walking up a deserted Fairfax Avenue, and that will never happen again. That opportunity won't transpire under normal circumstances. All the particulars that went into that. It was only possible on those nights. And I would be on a video phone date. My date would be inside their apartment. They wouldn't be leaving their apartment these days, and I would walk around because there was no one else walking around: zero people but me on Fairfax Avenue at night.

Everyone who lives in Los Angeles contributes to the idea that Los Angeles is paradise. And I get into this problem: I want my life to feel like paradise. But I can't be someone else while I'm busy being myself, and I am trying to tell you: my life doesn't feel shaped like a traditional narrative, my life feels shaped like me, and it could be paradise but it isn't. My life is a series of not so bad I wish I was deads and not so great it feels easies.

When they're open on Friday afternoons during the pandemic—when there isn't a quarantine lockdown—we dine on the outside patio of Connie & Ted's. How we accomplish this: we wear a mask and have our temperature taken before entering; they offer hand sanitizer. Hand sanitizer is everywhere these days. This charming seafood restaurant faces Santa Monica Boulevard, with a MedMen cannabis dispensary across the street, and when here it really feels like you're in West Hollywood; the waiters are so nice, too. Extraordinarily friendly waiters. I am here with my boss who is my friend, and he selected this place as part of our standard dining routine: we're in a place we want to be, about to eat food we want to eat.

The life of my boss-friend is devoted to reading literary fiction and poetry, because it's his job, and he calls it his dream job. I am friends with a man who deserves his dream life related to literary fiction and poetry, and he couldn't figure out how to speak with me about my recent book, which is the reality I am further accepting today at Connie & Ted's, while he further accepts the reality of not being able to speak with me about my book; a man of words, these words escape him; I feel distant from him, but I am making my way back. If the words aren't there, the words aren't there, and our relationship is reinforced by this combo: he's my boss *and* friend.

Three years with him and I am not now closer to the literature industry, I am in the same place I was—an outsider in an industry super serious about the Greeks, Shakespeare, and (bare minimum) college education. For understandable reasons, geniuses who convert their genius into literature flourish in the literature industry: and I am no genius. Nor have I been trained since my youth like a hugely successful ballerina or pianist. This industry is not built to accept me. But there are other ways to dance and play the piano and write books, anyway; the visible spectrum of an emotional world is endless, in my opinion.

He orders oysters and clams, shrimp, onion rings and a salad. I order fish and chips, substituting macaroni and cheese for the chips. He'll pay for my meal, and it will not be when I am older and this is gone from me that I appreciate these work meals: I appreciate them right fucking now. And I appreciate my boss. He is like me like this: life sure seems better in books. We both commit ourselves to the salvation offered by good writing, and we both consider life a whole lot of a whole lot; when he speaks with me about his personal life I listen, although I can't quite speak with him about my personal life.

Neither of us have mentioned him not bringing up my book. I am accepting it by myself. And I believe in him as a person regardless of everything else. And he believes in me as a person regardless of everything else, too. We order dessert. Me: a slice of apple pie with a scoop of vanilla ice cream. Him: a sundae glass of coffee ice cream with a scoop of chocolate sorbet atop. I want to fix everything bad in our lives, he wants to fix everything bad in our lives, and mainly we discuss the show and hang out.

Kazuo Ishiguro will be on the show soon: a Nobel Laureate. I appreciate this job while I have it. Where will this job lead me? The host says I might take over as host after he retires, but that's friendly daydreaming. Could I even do the show he does? When would I write? And the books he doesn't like, you'd never know it on the show. He'd never admit it. And I couldn't read a book that couldn't consume me. He is talented at letting books consume him, and explaining why. He mentions everything good about a book for the sake of the show, which is why it's especially awkward to me that he can't speak with me about my book. But as I say: nothing human disgusts me. It's a Tennessee Williams quote. When I quote Tennessee Williams around my boss-friend, he thinks I should quote someone besides Tennessee Williams. He isn't into southern melodrama. Southern melodrama is part of my bloodline.

Robert Johnson, Jr. is about to be on the show; on Monday we'll tape the conversation. He writes poetic southern prose in ways that make me weak-kneed. To help bolster his own appreciation, I tell my boss-friend about my appreciation of *The Prophets*—how it moves me, and how the philosophical size of its paragraphs inspires me. My boss-friend listens.

He has brought along his shopping list. There are three places I'll visit: a grocery store, a deli, and a fancy grocery store. I'll pick up items I'm familiar with picking up.

Now I'm at the grocery store, and before entering I call the deli.

I make my way through the grocery store, then I pick up the deli food, and then I walk to the fancy grocery store in my boss's neighborhood, stopping along my way to mail a Medicare payment at a post office.

Then I'm back home speaking with my internet movie friends about movie things that seem super important that day, although a week later none of it mattered in the first place.

For dinner I walk to Chipotle Mexican Grill and order a chicken burrito. I often visit better burrito places but Chipotle is in the neighborhood so it happens.

After dinner I am in the back alley of my apartment building, drinking high gravity malt liquor because I already ate my daily indica edibles and spent time letting my thoughts enter a writing zone. If you can believe it, and it's easy to believe because I'm into southern melodrama: everything that was just mentioned leads up to my writing this very chapter. I am writing this chapter right now: this is live footage. And maybe I could better write about this day another day, but then I would be writing about how the memory of the day feels, instead of how the day itself felt.

Specific complications spontaneously mentioned: I am not the same as most other people, but neither am I against most other people; I like things that most people don't like, and usually when most people like the same things as me it's not for the same reason.

Old dude wearing a long-sleeve yellow t-shirt and holding a bottle of beer in a photo on his book cover: also wearing some funny fishing hat and glasses, smiling. It's the author, Sam Pickering: *One Grand, Sweet Song*, Texas Review Press. This interests me in theory. Oh fascinating: he's the inspiration for the teacher in the movie *Dead Poets Society*, which was released when I was five. I recognized its impressive qualities when I saw it as a teenager, and I felt the movie understood me: directed by Peter Weir, with Robin Williams as the Sam Pickering-type. I had never heard of Sam Pickering and Texas Review Press isn't exactly a publishing company I'm familiar with. What about when you're living the dream and Texas Review Press publishes you. What about when you're the epitome of literature and Texas Review Press publishes you. Is that where the dream is, and where epitome lives? Why not? I hold this book and ponder the difference between what I know and what I need to know. I don't believe that everything that's wonderful is sufficiently acknowledged. Though I never get around to reading *One Grand, Sweet Song*, I must confess.

Work emails that remind me of myself: "I'm not sure who could understand me but you," emails sent to the host of a radio show about literary fiction and poetry, "no one understands my writing so I have encountered professional challenges," and "I believe in personal perseverance but wow it would be helpful if you would support me," and "I honestly suspect myself to be great but no one has noticed," and "I think differently than normal people do," and "I think about William Gass and Susan Sontag," and "I like all of your shows so we understand each other," and "I've written fourteen books but I haven't received any media coverage," and "no one wants to publish me but will you read me and recommend an editor," and "will you recommend an agent," and "will you write a blurb," and "the world has given up on me," and I could write so much of what I read from others, having the same problems they have, yet I am aware of the fact that these specific emails aren't going to solve their problems, and this show of established and prestigious writers isn't for them. What will we do and how will we do it?

This whole book could have been written with the intention of building up to this chapter in which I confess that I am my mother's son, but it happened in an organic manner owing to my writing style. My writing guided itself to this point beyond a breaking point: a revelation.

My mother and I lived in the house on the hill in the country when she wrote her first book, and one night by accident I deleted some of the pages from our family computer: she felt furious and I felt regretful. She told me she had first written those pages on yellow legal paper, so I copied those pages back onto the computer. The result was fewer pages than she said she had lost, so I felt sympathy for what I hadn't recovered. I hoped those pages were still in her head. I was between fifteen and seventeen when this took place, about twenty years ago. My mother's first book was *One Little Black Book*, and I thought it had such a lovely cover. It was a book about her childhood, and I read from it what I copied back onto the computer; some of her family members didn't consider the story fully accurate, and I am aware that my mother possesses an elaborate imagination in active pursuit of an ordinary explanation for why she is an abnormal person. I am aware that her writing corresponds to a point outside of reality, inside of her—I know that my mother writes her feelings, and narrative form is not the same as emotional form; though she did not attend a school for literature, my mother feels free to call herself a writer, because she thinks anyone who needs to write can. Looking up *One Little Black Back* on Goodreads.com right now, I see that it has a five-star rating, and the two ratings are from my mother. She paid to have it published, and I still think it's a great cover:

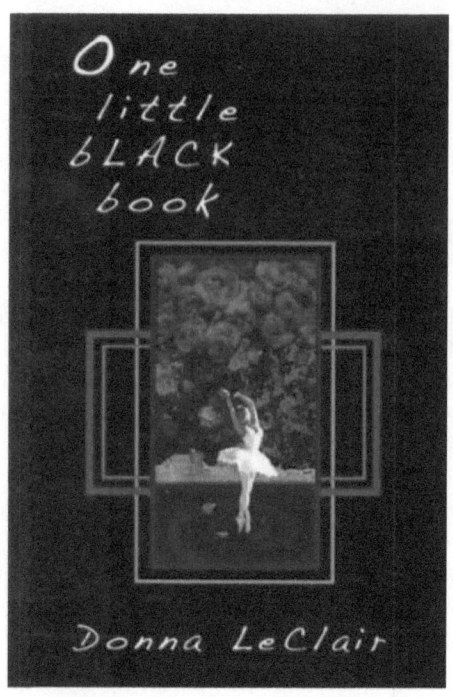

What do you think of her last name? She kept it after the divorce; she might have married for the last name.

When we moved to Orange County my mother first worked as a Hallmark store manager, which was the least she deserved, based on her entrepreneurial experience. During this time she wrote her second book, *WAKING REALITY: Overcoming the Heartache of Abuse.*

Soon after she became an assistant to an elite figure in Hollywood, and she converted this experience into her third book, *IMMUNITY: Entitlement of Wealthy Political Notables,* which she self-published, just as I was doing with my books by then. I couldn't speak with my mother about what I thought about her book that I couldn't bring myself to read. I had heard a scene at a sex party involves a dog, and she had witnessed this scene in real life. Heavy. She had thought about taking the sex party scene out, but her friend had said to leave the craziest scene in, think of *Pulp Fiction*. What friendly advice.

I wanted the best for my mother, of course, I wanted people to want her book, for sure. In fact I would pray for this at night: please let her readers exist, whoever they may be. Let the people who believe in her multiply: I'd look the other way and hope something good was happening.

By the time I was working for the literary fiction and poetry radio show, and writing my book *Gem City*, my mother had written her next book, INCH BY INCH: Flaws. Hauntings. Triumphs. I helped her set this one up for publication, by checking the page format and whatnot. What happens in this book is my mother enters a movie theater in which she recognizes the movie on the screen as her own life, and she already knows this story, so she leaves that screen to check on other screens showing the lives of other women: Helen Keller, Maya Angelou, Anne Frank, a few more. The topic is strong women. My mother quoted reference material for descriptions of the lives of these accomplished women, and wouldn't I do the same? Haven't I seen it done by writers in my generation? She was making up the idea of herself as a writer, taking certain drastic measures, and neither of us knew where she was headed: there is always a thrill in the unknown.

My mother. The strongest person I've ever witnessed. My mother. Her belief in herself keeps her going. My mother. A social outcast and the queen of my heart. My mother. Would I call her a good writer? I'd change the subject. I'd pretend like I didn't hear the question. I'd say anything but yes, except for no. I'd never say no. It wouldn't be me who said such. Would I say her heart was in this? I'd say it twice. She says she writes for therapy. She doesn't see a therapist, she writes. She is basically insane. She is off the map, mmhmm. Her radar is broken and she writes for God knows who and God knows why. She is me and I am her. She says she needs space to write. She says she writes to get away and find herself. She writes to flee life and discover it. She writes based on her own rules and what the hell. It doesn't matter what's wrong about what she writes: it matters if she stays alive to write, which she does. My mother. My hero. My mother. The sturdiest love I've ever known. My mother. The writer. After my boss-friend had shared the manuscript to *Gem City* with New Directions Publishing, and they didn't want to have anything to do with it—or bring it up in conversation with me, they ignored it—and I understood what happened, it was okay that they weren't looking for me—I had been fortunate to even experience the submission—and I wouldn't be a published writer on the show I worked for, I also couldn't get my mother on the show, for reasons I couldn't explain to her, same as I couldn't explain the reasons I couldn't be on the show to myself. My mother. I love her.

You may have noticed, and it was previously mentioned: I become so serious about some topics often. And it really does seem best to become serious only about what's constructive. Serious about solutions. Because otherwise your seriousness just notices or worse, worsens, problems. I'm speaking to myself. Ruminating upon all those times in my life my perspective or feelings have slipped away from me, and my thoughts have traveled with them. True story: my thoughts can slip so far away from me that it can take me one or six days to recover them. I used to want to write to express my existential despair with earnest conviction, but I don't think that's constructive. And my existentialism isn't often right. I'm often screaming when I could be singing. Why choose to scream? I have thus described the traditional emotional shape of all my books and stories, including this one. They're always about overcoming sorrow I encounter and create. Despair I conjure and surmount. If I make any of this look easy, my god. You see: I struggle to find a stable perspective in a rational world that doesn't need me. And because I so regularly engage in these struggles is why I'm proud of when I stabilize. I always think: after stability arrives, a quiet ending. I treasure quiet endings. Tranquility. Lifted burdens. A dance beneath an interior mountain of frustration. I might be the one who makes the mountain but I'm also the one who lifts it. I can't change every bit of my reality but I can change every bit of my perspective. And if I could stabilize every normal day I'd have more normal days. And if I could do that at the beginning of a book I'd have a more traditional narrative. I like the expression, This is the way God made me. I like believing that my flaws and imperfections are part of my design. I don't mean that as an excuse for them, no, and I don't believe that I shouldn't work on correcting myself, and building myself as a person, no I'm not saying that. I'm just saying I like the expression This is the way God made me, and I'm not sure if I'll ever fix all that needs fixed. I doubt it, sincerely. I'm mainly working on writing better books. So this is me, and what about this.

My reaction to the movies *Fast Cars Fast Women* (1981) and *Starship Eros* (1979):

These are two bona fide genre movies that are also adult movies, both written/directed by Scott McHaley, the only two movies he ever wrote/directed (which makes them more impressive from my perspective).

This was my first dip into Vinegar Syndrome's Peekarama series and great, now the bar is raised for that entire series.

I began with *Fast Cars Fast Women* because it's at the top of the dvd menu screen, although in fact this was made after *Starship Eros*.

Okay: what an impressive and authentic portrait of a southern race car driver's reality. What total immersion into a southern lifestyle in general: early on when you see the race track I thought, nice, but by the time we're in a bar with a live county-western band performing I'm becoming impressed. Although a potential sibling to this movie would be *The Legend of Billie Jean*, the bar scene is *Nashville*-level. It feels like I'm in a bear hearing a live band perform. Verisimilitude. Still an adult movie, however, a slight distinction exists in this song lyric, "Slide on in, darling I'm so what you're looking for," and although in a lyrical context you could justify that the singer is referring to a hug, I mean.

This is a fully formed movie, although yes it's an adult movie. That combination is assuredly accomplished. So there's a rivalry between the owners of race cars, one female and one male, and their rivalry is spiked by the fact that the evil male-owner also runs a company in financial trouble. He wants to win prize movie to pay off his debts. And he's so evil he tampered with a car that crashed and killed its driver. The star of this movie is a woman who arrives to replace that dead team member. She will drive the same car that killed its previous driver. Wow. The stakes are high. Damn. And what transpires is a deft amalgamation of this narrative and sex scenes.

You go from the evil male-owner visiting the holy female-owner, and the female-owner won't put out to him of course (she sleeps with her pit boss), so she masturbates while the evil male-owner watches. And next you witness thugs in cheap winter masks attack the pit boss. Followed by a female-and-female shower scene. This is how the movie progresses.

The evil male-owner wants to overpower the holy female-owner, but he is way, way underestimating her strength and ability. She confronts him in a pit and tells him, "Stay away from my wheels. Stay away from my girls. If you don't I'm going to chop your balls off," and we hear the click of her heels as she walks away.

A main goon on the evil side is Ron Jeremy, back when he was young and possessed beauty imo. You see him doing goon stuff and you see a car crash. What, appropriate for this movie, doesn't this movie offer me? It absolutely works car fetishization into the movie at a John Frankenheimer's *Grand Prix*-level. You see closeups of car stuff before the final race, when everything is on the line. The movie ends with a car race and it's pretty much a perfect movie. The disc offers soft core outtakes taken from sex scenes. Somehow: all of this is real. This is reality. The movie trailer is another special future.

Starship Eros begins with a video of the producer as a special feature. He says Scott McHaley wrote the script and showed it to him, and the producer was like, yeah for sure. And it was financed through stunt men. The producer says he directed the sex scenes because McHaley was so fresh. But you're wrong if you think McHaley didn't make his own significant contributions: he made the movie's special effects in his garage, and I assume he directed the scenes of space chases and space battles.

The producer says it was a two-day shoot and I wonder how they did that.

The first shot is a star-filled sky from the perspective of space travel. The year's title card appears: we're in the future of 1995.

How they accomplished the two-day shoot is this movie has the narrative speed of porn, yet also you are in space. The first ten minutes establish who the commander is: we're introduced to her through a hot tub scene, followed by self-pleasure, followed by intercourse. Then we're in the special effects of space: we can see a space station, and a flying spaceship. A pilot arrives at a space station and a woman greets her, tells her, "Beverly here, everyone calls me Bev." This ship is women-only. Though there is a sex robot named Quasar, played by a man wearing a C-3PO mask. You see his hands and later his penis. He says he's human from the waist down (although as mentioned you also see his human hands). He wears a robot vest. With the mask and vest he looks like a robot, count it.

When the captain meets the commander you learn about the spaceship lifestyle: "Sorry to interrupt commander, I didn't know this was pleasure period." The commander had been self-pleasuring. But not upset at all, the commander says, "Strip and do me." These crew members are super nice to each other. Real friends.

While meeting Quasar through sex, the pilot encounters a situation in which Quasar's battery loses power and must be replaced. Good detail, space sex movie.

They're called into mission 28 min into the 67 min movie, and it does feel like one shooting day has transpired. It's miraculous how little happens in this movie that also feels like a complete-enough movie. Called into a mission, suddenly the sex actors are controlling a spaceship. The mission pertains to the daring Amazoids up to extreme mischief. Starship Eros is in pursuit.

"Think we'll see any action, commander?"

"It isn't very likely we won't."

In order to change into combat gear, the pilot leaves the flight deck, although while changing she sees Quasar and becomes distracted, for which she's later punished.

Sex scenes are intercut with scenes of spaceflight. Damn, Scott McHaley, you really know how to treat a movie. *Fast Cars Fast Women* fetishizes cars and this movie fetishizes sci-fi. The pilot's punishment for becoming distracted by Quasar during a mission is the wildest punishment I've ever witnessed in a movie, involving a laser gun and manual stimulation. The punishment makes the pilot sweat.

Again, very little has happened, but enough to call it a movie, and plenty to call it adult. 55min into the movie the enemy captain is captured. By this point Bev is walking around naked. Accomplishments at the end of the movie are Quasar comes on his own (without programming, his first time), and the enemy captain is converted into a team member.

Only God knows why I was born in the United States of America, I ended up at a Seventh-day Adventist high school because of my neighbors, and I adored Ohio, although I sensed that more existed: I wanted more from life than what it gave me, and so I went searching for more, slowly and badly, first guessing at my path through the adult world by attending a Seventh-day Adventist university—I told them I wanted to be a park ranger, and they recommended a degree in horticulture. A short while later I landed in California with my dreams in a suitcase, although this world didn't dress itself in my dreams. My twenties, fuck them. Or no, they were okay. But they weren't one thing to the next: not even close. They were formless, blob-like; amorphous. My thirties began with optimism because my childish dreams hadn't evaporated by then; now I'm thirty-seven and, oh, it was my childhood that evaporated. And I have strayed so far from a proper path in the adult world: reality has been a buzzkill. Reality has harshed my experience at only living once. My life consists of constant questions instead of easy answers. Why anything? Writing about my life is my way of creating life outside of me: the theme of my life is perseverance, apparently, possibly general interior strength, although these qualities have always been present in me, and just now they're rather central. Though the world doesn't care about what keeps me going. One writes for what one wants to read, and although I talk big-game about books, in fact I prefer people; since I have not encountered myself as a person in a book, this is up to me. I suppose my favorite people are messy because I am. My favorite lives are trash lives far too bland to be significant, because I consider that highly relatable. There is no meaning to this book, it's all about blowing kisses to existence. My favorite book and movie characters sass universal meaning, and my favorite struggles to witness are achingly ordinary, daily struggles of minor significance. It's a taste thing: I don't want to read about a character in a story, I want to read about a person who has the strength it takes for a life in this world, with ethereal themes and disjointed plot mechanics. Hell, I appreciate sunlight more than I appreciate traditional narratives. The sun gives life and traditional stories imitate it. This is my real life that someone might say is not that interesting—rude.

Bananas: I have to accept the likelihood of a future in which a robot will write a book about feeling human.

I'm listening to music from the *Nomadland* soundtrack because last night I watched that movie with the woman I previously mentioned. I'm feeling saturated with the Golden Age of Porn so I needed to watch something contemporary—observe the interests of current normal people. She has Hulu so there we go. This chapter is more live footage, and the song is titled "Oltremare," which probably means something. Okay. It's a beautiful song. I'm listening to it from a YouTube page that repeats it for over an hour. What's ephemeral and what's lasting? Besides science stuff, I'm not sure. How do I feel tonight? I'm sure how I feel tonight, and what moves me is elegant piano songs. I haven't finished reading Richard Brautigan's *The Abortion* but I will soonish. I worry that his prose doesn't enrich me enough. I worry that simple prose wouldn't impress you enough. I worry that my life isn't impressive enough, that my thoughts aren't impressive enough, that I don't experience enough emotions, and that I'm not pretty enough. But I'm over my worries right now, which is how every one of my narratives ends. Not with everything fixed, nah. No, never that. The only thing I fix by the end of each narrative is my worries. Personally, calm depressing endings calm me.

Do you ever say something and later feel embarrassed by it? That's how I currently feel about previously mentioning that I prefer tranquil endings: how tame. And if I never disagree with myself, I'll never change. Let me not be tame at the end of this book: I'm sipping from a teacup inhabited by a pod of dolphins, but dolphins swimming through my esophagus aren't the ending either. If I were a dolphin my snout would be bottle shaped and that statement is irrelevant, though it's nearer to the conversation than a non sequitur. Even the imagination has its limits. I've previously ended my books with fantasy but I'm kind of over that, like epigraphs. Maybe not forever but at least for now.

For some reason I possess a certain kinetic energy, and I would say the powerhouse of that energy is my soul, though someone might ask me what my soul is. I didn't say I would answer. Art evokes the ephemeral and I write about my life as art. The truth is I've never wanted to be anything but reckless, and the controllable disturbs me. The understandable snores me. Though nonconformity is still a title, and I'll die incomplete. I'll die in the middle of a sentence. I conform to the idea that words can unlock people, and I unlock myself with words. You are made of the same human materials I am. We possess the same existential ingredients. This book is exactly what I wanted it to be, needed it to be. It is true that who best understands why that is is me, now, as I write this book, but may I have left enough of myself behind to be understood by others. This book is not fully perfect but it is fully me, which is cooler in my opinion. I act upon principle, and I answer my own questions. I ascertain my own significance. Thank you. The future doesn't need me, no one requires me or the things I love, so I feel the need to love myself and the things I love: I'm standing in my apartment's back alley drinking malt liquor at night, which isn't recommended. I'm thirty-seven and I am my own life plan. I'm making hysterical statements in a fever dream. I'm walking behind your eyelids. I live in your imagination. I'm singing inside myself while screaming at you. I wouldn't be being my true self if I did it any other way. These are cataclysmic words on purpose, from a person who is the mystery of why he can be none other.

Backlit igloos and walruses in on the joke.

www.ingramcontent.com/pod-product-compliance
Lightning Source LLC
Chambersburg PA
CBHW031429210526
45464CB00005B/2121